Vocabulary *Tales*™

I Think I Need a Pet

by Pamela Chanko
illustrated by Kelly Kennedy

SCHOLASTIC INC.

New York • Toronto • London • Auckland • Sydney
Mexico City • New Delhi • Hong Kong • Buenos Aires

Designed by Maria Lilja
ISBN-13: 978-0-545-08867-1 • ISBN-10: 0-545-08867-4
Copyright © 2008 by Scholastic Inc.
All rights reserved. Printed in China.

SCHOLASTIC, VOCABULARY TALES™, and associated logos are trademarks and/or registered trademarks of Scholastic Inc.

First printing, November 2008

12 11 10 9 8 7 6 5 4 3 2 1   8 9 10 11 12 13/0

Building Vocabulary With This Book

This book contains eight key words that are important for all children to know. Read the story straight through for enjoyment. Then read it again, pausing to define and discuss each key word. Follow-up the tale with the fun activities on pages 14–16. When you're done, celebrate—kids will have added eight great words to their vocabularies!

"We're going to the zoo today," said Daddy.
"Good," I said. "I think I need a pet. The zoo will be a good place to find one."
Daddy thought I was wrong.

First we saw the lions. A **fierce** lion could scare away the monsters under my bed. "I think I need a pet lion," I said. But Daddy thought I was wrong.

3

KEY WORD: **trunk**

Simple Definition: the long nose of an elephant

Sample Sentence: An elephant sucks up water through its *trunk* and then sprays the water into its mouth to drink.

Next we saw the elephants. An elephant's **trunk** could help me water the plants.

"I think I need a pet elephant," I said.

But Daddy thought I was wrong.

KEY WORD: **gallop**

Simple Definition: to run very fast, like a horse

Sample Sentence: I love to watch the horses *gallop* around the racetrack.

Then we saw the zebras. I could ride a zebra to school.
It would **gallop** fast and get me there on time.
"I think I need a pet zebra," I said.
But Daddy thought I was wrong.

KEY WORD: humongous

Simple Definition: very, very, very big

Sample Sentence: We went to the movies and got a *humongous* tub of popcorn at the snack bar.

Next we saw the hippos. A **humongous** hippo could help me finish my dinner when I'm too full.

"I think I need a pet hippo," I said.

But Daddy thought I was wrong.

Then we saw the giraffes. A giraffe could get things that are too high for me to reach.
"I think I need a pet giraffe," I said.
But Daddy thought I was wrong.

"You do not need a **wild** animal," Daddy said.

KEY WORD: tame

Simple Definition: to take an animal from the wild and train it to live with people

Sample Sentence: A leopard is not a good pet, because you could not *tame* it.

"But I could **tame** it," I said.

Daddy still thought I was wrong.

"Come on," he said. "It's time to go home."

KEY WORD: habitat

Simple Definition: the place where a plant or animal normally lives and grows

Sample Sentence: The ocean is a whale's natural *habitat*.

Daddy said our house was not a good **habitat** for a lion or a zebra or a giraffe. I was sad. Then we saw some dogs and cats that needed homes.

"Look, Daddy!" I said.

"Well, what do you know," he replied.

KEY WORD: veterinarian

Simple Definition: a doctor who takes care of animals

Sample Sentence: When my cat got sick, the *veterinarian* helped make her better.

"Hello. I think I need a pet," I said.

"How about this little puppy?" asked the lady.

"We found him on the street. He's been to the **veterinarian**, and he's very healthy."

"He has no one to take care of him," I told Daddy.
"I don't need all those other animals. But this one
needs me!"

And guess what? Daddy thought I was right!

Meaning Match

Listen to the definition. Then go to the WORD CHEST and find a vocabulary word that matches it.

1 the long nose of an elephant

2 living in nature; not taken care of by humans

3 the place where a plant or animal normally lives

4 a doctor who takes care of animals

5 to take an animal from the wild and train it to live with people

6 strong and dangerous

7 very, very, very big

8 to run very fast

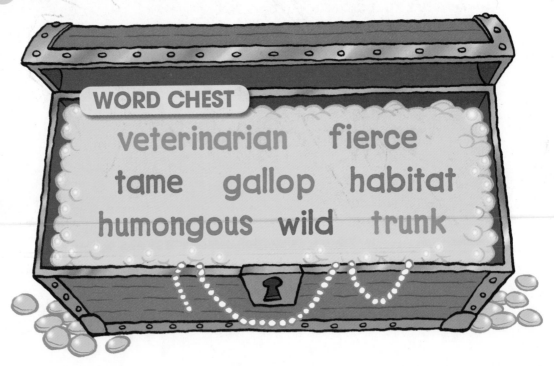

WORD CHEST

veterinarian   fierce
tame   gallop   habitat
humongous   wild   trunk

Answers: 1. trunk 2. wild 3. habitat 4. veterinarian 5. tame 6. fierce 7. humongous 8. gallop

Vocabulary Fill-ins

Listen to the sentence. Then go to the WORD BOX and find the best word to fill in the blank.

WORD BOX

habitat	tame	fierce	veterinarian
humongous	wild	gallop	trunk

1 I wish that I could _____ a tiger and turn it into a loving pet.

2 I was so hungry that I ate a _____ bowl of spaghetti all by myself.

3 The horse ran faster and faster until it began to _____.

4 The desert is a natural _____ for many snakes and lizards.

5 An elephant can pick up peanuts with its _____.

6 Raccoons, birds, and squirrels are just a few _____ animals you may see right in your own backyard.

7 The _____ gives my dog a check-up once a year.

8 The mother bear became _____ when she thought her cub was in trouble.

Answers: 1. tame 2. humongous 3. gallop 4. habitat 5. trunk 6. wild 7. veterinarian 8. fierce

Vocabulary Questions

Listen to each question. Think about it. Then answer.

1. What animals are **humongous**? Make a list.

2. What is your favorite **wild** animal? Why?

3. Why might a person need to take a pet to the **veterinarian**? What could the **veterinarian** do for the pet?

4. What animals are easy to **tame**? What animals are hard to **tame**?

5. Would you like to have a long **trunk** like an elephant? How would you use it?

6. Would you like to be riding on a horse when it started to **gallop**? Why or why not?

7. Can you make a **fierce** face? Give it a try!

8. Pretend you are your favorite animal. What is your **habitat**? Describe it and tell why you like to live there.

Extra: Can you think of some more animal words? Make a list.